D0789218

A FIRST LOOK AT
SEALS, SEA LIONS,
AND WALRUSES

A FIRST LOOK AT SEALS, SEA LIONS, AND WALRUSES

By Millicent E. Selsam and Joyce Hunt

Illustrated by Harriett Springer

WALKER AND COMPANY ✹ NEW YORK

First published in the United States of America in 1988 by the Walker
Publishing Company, Inc.

Published simultaneously in Canada by Thomas Allen & Son,
Canada, Limited, Markham, Ontario

Library of Congress Cataloging-in-Publication Data

Selsam, Millicent Ellis, 1912–
    A first look at seals, sea lions, and walruses / by Millicent E.
Selsam and Joyce Hunt ; illustrated by Harriett Springer.
    p.   cm.—(A First look at series)
    Includes index.
    Summary: Compares and contrasts the physical characteristics,
habits, and natural environment of seals, sea lions, and walruses.
    ISBN 0-8027-6787-7. ISBN 0-8027-6788-5 (lib. bdg.)
    1. Seals—Juvenile literature. 2. Sea lions—Juvenile literature.
3. Walruses—Juvenile literature. [1. Seals. 2. Sea lions.
3. Walruses.] I. Hunt, Joyce. II. Springer, Harriett, ill.
III. Title. IV. Series: Selsam, Millicent Ellis, 1912–   First look
at series.
QL737.P6S43   1988   87-29491
599.74′5—dc19   CIP
                                                        AC

Printed in the United States of America

10 9 8 7 6 5 4 3 2 1

A *FIRST LOOK AT* SERIES

A FIRST LOOK AT LEAVES
A FIRST LOOK AT FISH
A FIRST LOOK AT MAMMALS
A FIRST LOOK AT BIRDS
A FIRST LOOK AT INSECTS
A FIRST LOOK AT FROGS AND TOADS
A FIRST LOOK AT SNAKES, LIZARDS, AND OTHER REPTILES
A FIRST LOOK AT ANIMALS WITH BACKBONES
A FIRST LOOK AT ANIMALS WITHOUT BACKBONES
A FIRST LOOK AT FLOWERS
A FIRST LOOK AT THE WORLD OF PLANTS
A FIRST LOOK AT MONKEYS AND APES
A FIRST LOOK AT SHARKS
A FIRST LOOK AT WHALES
A FIRST LOOK AT CATS
A FIRST LOOK AT DOGS
A FIRST LOOK AT HORSES
A FIRST LOOK AT SEASHELLS
A FIRST LOOK AT DINOSAURS
A FIRST LOOK AT SPIDERS
A FIRST LOOK AT ROCKS
A FIRST LOOK AT BIRD NESTS
A FIRST LOOK AT KANGAROOS, KOALAS,
    AND OTHER ANIMALS WITH POUCHES
A FIRST LOOK AT OWLS, EAGLES, AND OTHER
    HUNTERS OF THE SKY
A FIRST LOOK AT POISONOUS SNAKES
A FIRST LOOK AT CATERPILLARS
A FIRST LOOK AT SEALS, SEA LIONS, AND WALRUSES

Each of the nature books in this series is planned to develop the child's powers of observation—to train him or her to notice distinguishing characteristics. A leaf is a leaf. A bird is a bird. An insect is an insect. That is true. But what makes an oak leaf different from a maple leaf? Why is a hawk different from an eagle, or a beetle different from a bug?

Classification is a painstaking science. These books give a child the essence of the search for differences that is the basis for scientific classification.

For Sadie

The authors wish to thank Mr. Kenneth Chambers of the American Museum of Natural History for reading the text of this book.

Seals have flippers and swim in the sea.

Are they fish?

flippers

flippers

No, they are mammals because they have hair or fur, and their babies nurse on the mother's milk.

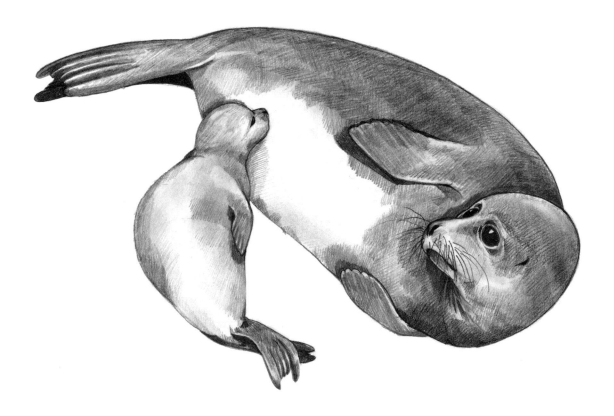

Fish have no hair.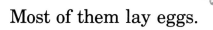

Most of them lay eggs.

In the sea, seals streak through the water.

On land they are clumsy. They waddle and wriggle
as they move from place to place.

How do you tell seals apart?

Some have tusks.
Some have spots.
Some have manes like those of lions.

Look at the heads of these two seals.

Which one has ears?

The seal with ears belongs to a group called *Eared Seals*.

The seal without ears belongs to a group called *True Seals*.

True seals and eared seals sit and move in different ways.

On land, most true seals cannot lift themselves up
on their small front flippers.

They move by dragging themselves along on their bellies.

On land, eared seals can lift themselves up
on their large front flippers.

They move by using their front and back flippers.

Many eared seals are called *Sea Lions*.

EARED SEALS

You can tell some eared seals apart by their size.
The smallest ones weigh about 140 lbs. (64 kg.).

Galapagos Fur Seal

The largest ones weigh
about 2200 lbs. (1000 kg.).

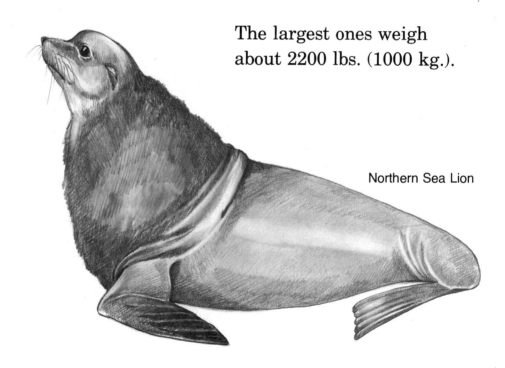

Northern Sea Lion

A male eared seal can be four times bigger
than the female.

Many males are dark.
Many females are white.

Hooker's Sea Lions

Sometimes the markings help tell one seal from another.

Here are two dark seals.

Find the one with light-colored fur
on its head and shoulders.

Find the one with light-colored fur
on its face and chest.

Australian Sea Lion

Sub-Antarctic Fur Seal

19

Here is the *California Sea Lion*.
This trained seal uses its nose to play ball.

TRUE SEALS

Here are some true seals lying on their bellies.

How do we tell one from another?

True seals can also be told by their markings.

Which seal has white bands on its body?

Which seal has a dark face and a dark band on its back?

Which seal has white circles on its back?

Harp Seal

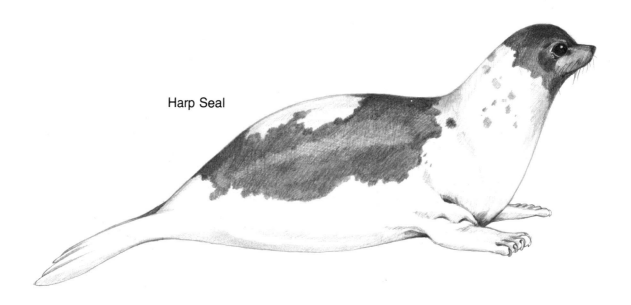

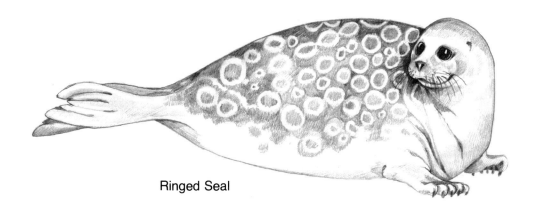

Ringed Seal

Ribbon Seal

23

Here are two seals with spots.
Weddell Seals are dark and have light spots.
Harbor Seals are light and have dark spots.

Which is which?

Here is another light-colored seal with dark spots.
But look at its funny nose.
It blows up like a balloon when the seal gets excited.

Hooded Seal

This seal also has an odd nose.

We don't know if it is called an *Elephant Seal* because it is so big or because it has such a long nose.

This seal has longer, thicker whiskers than other seals.

Bearded Seal

The babies of many true seals are white and wooly.

Harp Seal and Baby

Ribbon Seal and Baby

WALRUSES

The walrus is not an eared seal or a true seal.
It looks a little like both.

But a walrus has tusks and very little fur on its body.

Notice its stiff whiskers.

WHERE SEALS, SEA LIONS, AND WALRUSES CAN BE FOUND

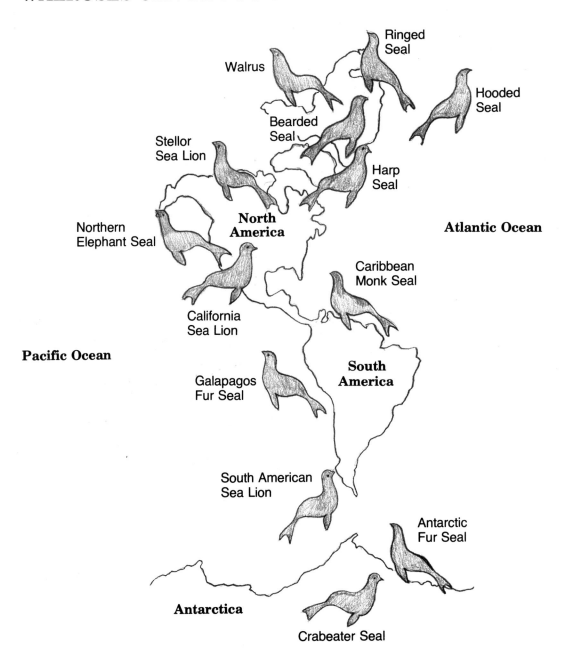

Ringed Seal

Walrus

Hooded Seal

Bearded Seal

Stellor Sea Lion

Harp Seal

Northern Elephant Seal

North America

Atlantic Ocean

Caribbean Monk Seal

California Sea Lion

Pacific Ocean

Galapagos Fur Seal

South America

South American Sea Lion

Antarctic Fur Seal

Antarctica

Crabeater Seal

Northern
Fur Seal

Harbor
Seal

Ribbon Seal

Northern
Elephant Seal

Europe

Gray Seal

Asia

Africa

Australia

Australian
Fur Seal
and
Sea Lion

Hooker's
Sea Lion

Antarctica

Weddell Seal

TO TELL EARED SEALS APART:

Look for ears.

Look at the way they sit.

Look at their size.

Look at their markings.

TO TELL TRUE SEALS APART:

Look at the way they sit.

Look at their markings.

Look for funny noses.

Look for whiskers.

TO TELL WALRUSES FROM SEALS:

Look for tusks.

SEALS, SEA LIONS, AND WALRUSES IN THIS BOOK